Soul Wounds for Daughters

Healing Mother Wounds:
A Journey of Reflection and Growth

Dear Beautiful Soul,

Sometimes, we may not have been able to converse honestly with our mothers for various reasons. We were afraid to ask some questions, and some they have declined to answer. Safe spaces may not have been created due to emotional unavailability or various insecurities. Unanswered questions can often leave us feeling stuck.

Healing a "mother" wound is essential for several reasons. It allows us to confront, heal, and understand the emotional pain that may have stemmed from those experiences. Acknowledging their existence, whether these wounds are abandonment, injustice, betrayal, rejection, or humiliation, is the first step to healing.

This journal was created with compassion for wounded daughters, whether adopted or raised by a grandmother, auntie, or other feminine energy, especially a deceased mother. Welcome to your safe place. You were brave enough to take the journey. Remember to be kind to yourself throughout this process. Remember that healing is a process, and it is not linear. Take as many breaks as often as needed if things get too emotional. It's your journey. You got this!

With compassion and encouragement,

Dr. Kellie Diane

Publisher Awareherness Press Publishers
Awareherness@gmail.com

ISBN: 978-1-965702-03-1

Unraveling the Threads

Day 1

Reflecting on the term "mother wound," what does it mean to you?

....
....
....
....
....
....
....
....
....
....
....
....
....
....
....
....

Day 2

What was your earliest memory of your mother? How does it make you feel?

Day 3

Mother-daughter relationships can be complicated. Describe a time when you felt unsupported. What emotions surfaced?

Day 4

Often, our mothers are our first example of femininity. List three qualities you admire in your mother. Why do they stand out?

Day 5

Reflect on your relationship and Write about a significant lesson you learned from your mother.

Day 6

What do you wish you could tell your mother about your feelings? Write down how you feel.

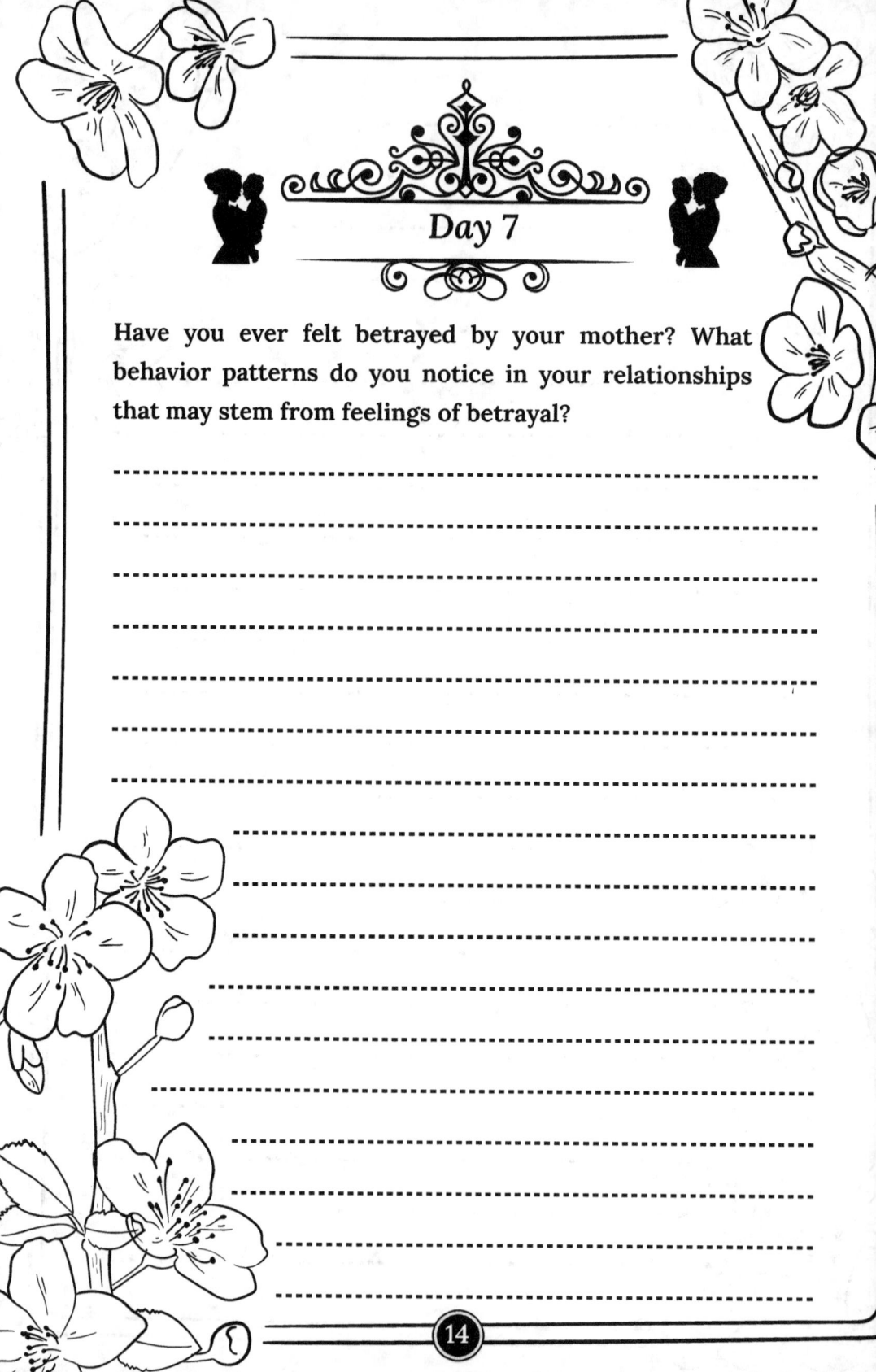

Day 7

Have you ever felt betrayed by your mother? What behavior patterns do you notice in your relationships that may stem from feelings of betrayal?

Day 8

Discuss your mother's parenting style, which can be sensitive. What impact has it had on you? Please feel free to share your thoughts and feelings.

Day 9

Though we may not believe it, we have made our mothers proud countless times. Can you share a moment when you felt incredibly proud of your fantastic mother? Share your story!

Day 10

Writing can be therapeutic. Compose a letter to your younger self discussing your relationship with your mother. Discuss how you can work through your wound of betrayal

----

Navigating your Emotions

Day 11

What feelings come to mind when you think about your relationship? Write them down.

....

....

....

....

....

....

....

....

....

....

....

....

....

....

....

Day 12

Can you recall a moment when you felt abandoned by your mother? Write down the moment and explain your feelings.

Day 13

I understand that conflicts with loved ones can be difficult. Can you share a time when you had a conflict with your mother and how it was resolved?

Day 14

When you think of your mothers, what emotions come to mind? Take some time to really delve into those feelings.

Day 15

Our mothers' actions may have sometimes impacted our self-esteem. Write down how you feel without critical judgment toward yourself.

Day 16

Feeling misunderstood by our mother can be challenging., Could you describe a specific instance when you experienced this.

Day 17

Coping mechanisms are often developed due to your past relationship with your mother. What coping mechanisms did you develop?

Day 18

How do you express love, and how does it relate to your mother's style?

....

....

....

....

....

....

....

....

....

....

....

....

....

....

....

....

....

Day 19

Describe a time when you felt truly connected to your mother. It can be a deeply personal and meaningful experience. Write down your experience.

Day 20

Write down three things you wish were different in your relationship with your mother.

Embracing Forgiveness

Day 21

Forgiveness is often not an easy process. What does forgiveness mean to you? Explore your thoughts.

Day 22

Though difficult, writing a letter of forgiveness to your mother can be a healing and empowering experience. After writing the letter, decide whether you will share it with her or keep it safely stored away. Whatever decision you make, be kind to yourself.

Day 23

Reflect on what you 5 things that you appreciate about
your mother.

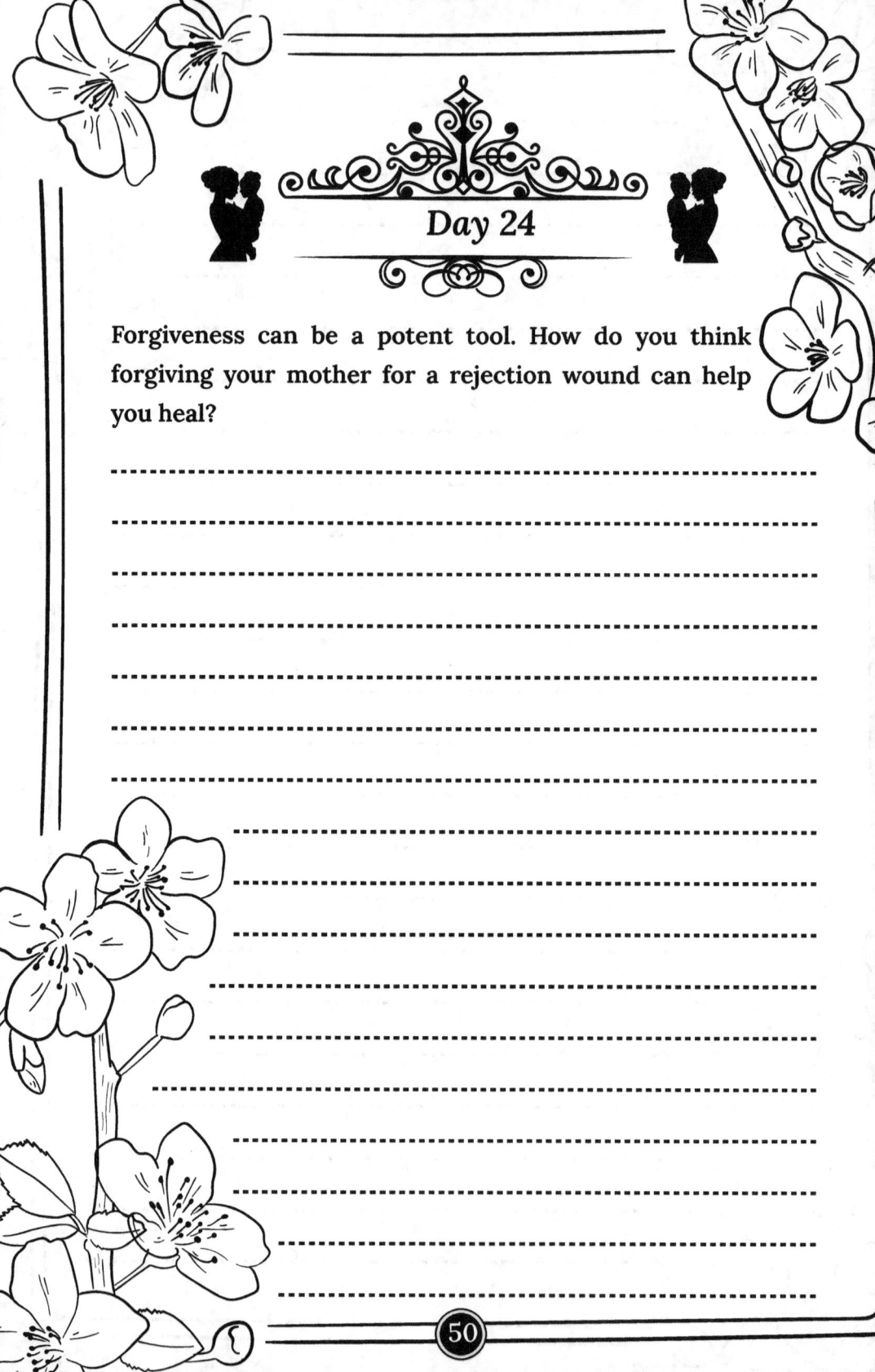

Day 24

Forgiveness can be a potent tool. How do you think forgiving your mother for a rejection wound can help you heal?

Day 25

Describe how you felt when your mother was not emotionally present for you. How did her absence impact your feelings of safety or belonging?

Day 26

Though difficult, write about how you can accept your mother as she is.

....
....
....
....
....
....
....
....
....
....
....
....
....
....
....
....

Day 27

Explore the idea of unconditional love. How does it apply to your relationship? Are you able to reciprocate the same unconditional love towards your mother?

Day 28

What boundaries do you need to set toward your mother for your emotional well-being?

....
....
....
....
....
....
....
....
....
....
....
....
....
....
....
....

Day 29

Write about a moment of joy you shared with your mother.

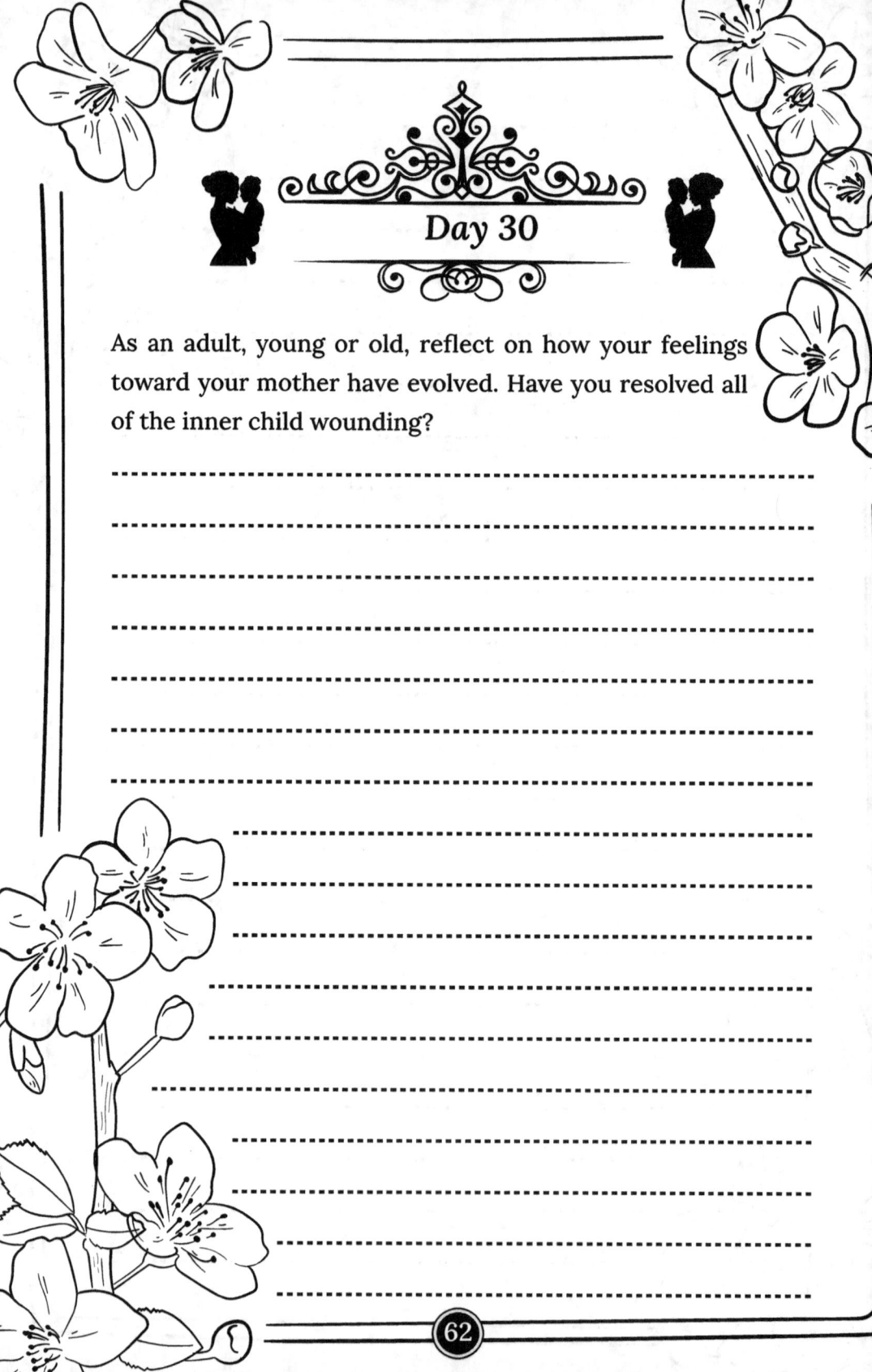

Day 30

As an adult, young or old, reflect on how your feelings toward your mother have evolved. Have you resolved all of the inner child wounding?

Finding Peace
Through Healing

Day 31

What self-care practices have you chosen today to promote healing from emotional wounds?

....
....
....
....
....
....
....
....
....
....
....
....
....
....
....
....

Day 32

Describe a self-care routine that brings you peace and comfort. If you haven't developed one, create one here

....

....

....

....

....

....

....

....

....

....

....

....

....

....

....

....

Day 33

How do you nurture your inner child to heal through the wounds of rejection, abandonment, betrayal, injustice, and humiliation?

Day 34

Name five mindfulness practices that help cope with emotions. How have you found them helpful?

....
....
....
....
....
....
....
....
....
....
....
....
....
....
....

Day 35

Healing can be enjoyable. Create a vision board for your healing journey.

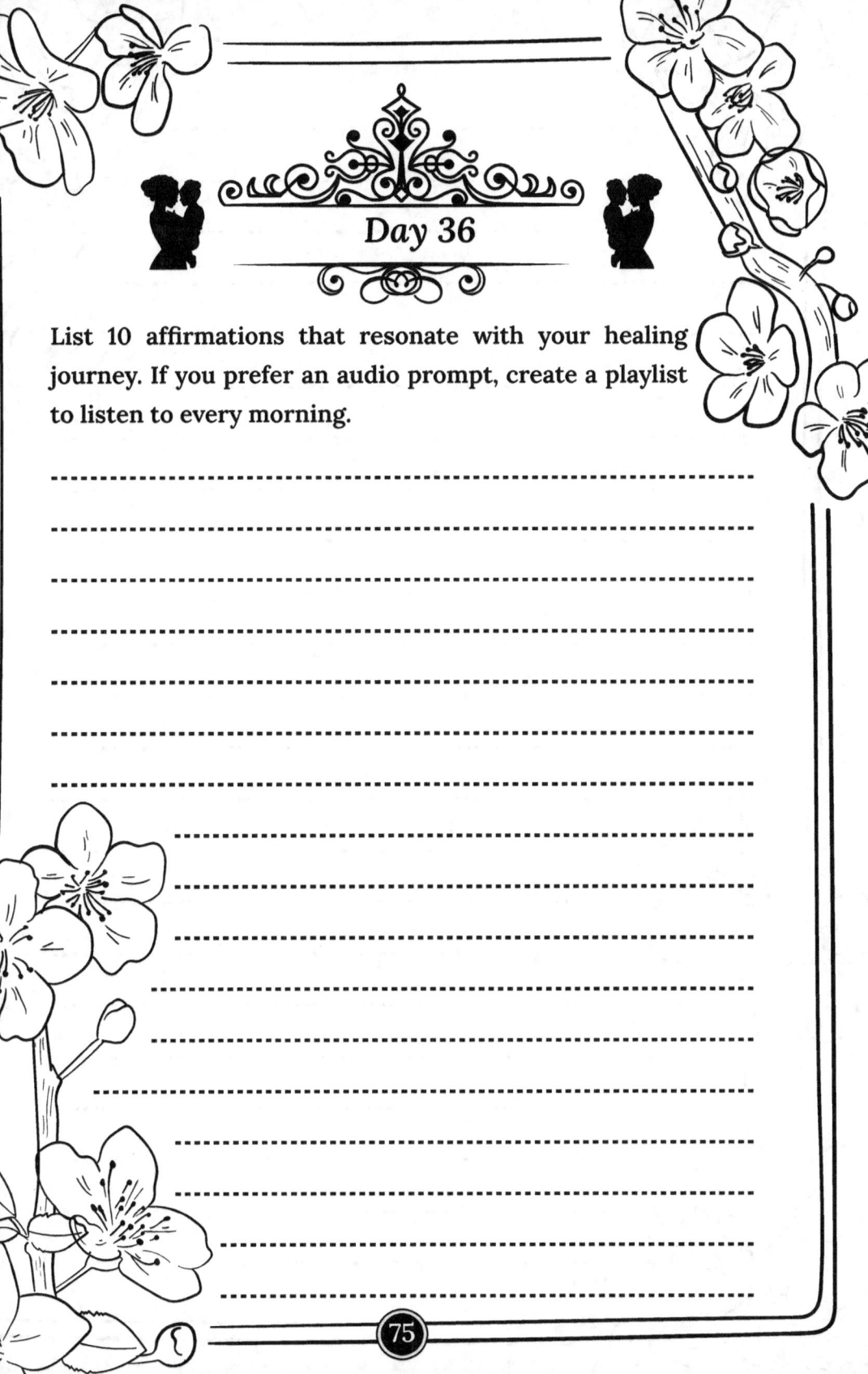

Day 36

List 10 affirmations that resonate with your healing
journey. If you prefer an audio prompt, create a playlist
to listen to every morning.

Day 37

What hobbies bring you joy? How can you incorporate them into your routine?

···
···
···
···
···
···
···
···
···
···
···
···
···
···
···

Day 38

Reflect on the significance of support systems in the healing process and identify your support network.

....
....
....
....
....
....
....
....
....
....
....
....
....
....
....
....

Day 39

Write about a book or resource that has helped you understand your feelings.

....
....
....
....
....
....
....
....
....
....
....
....
....
....
....
....

Day 40

Try a new activity that feels nurturing (e.g., yoga, art).
Reflect on the experience.

Embracing
Change

Day 41

What lessons have you learned from your experiences with your mother?

....
....
....
....
....
....
....
....
....
....
....
....
....
....
....
....

Day 42

How do you want your relationship with your mothers to evolve?

Day 43

Write about how you can communicate your needs more effectively.

....

....

....

....

....

....

....

....

....

....

....

....

....

....

....

....

Day 44

If you are a mom, write about the qualities you want to embody. If you aren't, what qualities would you like to have as a mom?

Day 45

Describe your hopes for the future of your mother-daughter relationship.

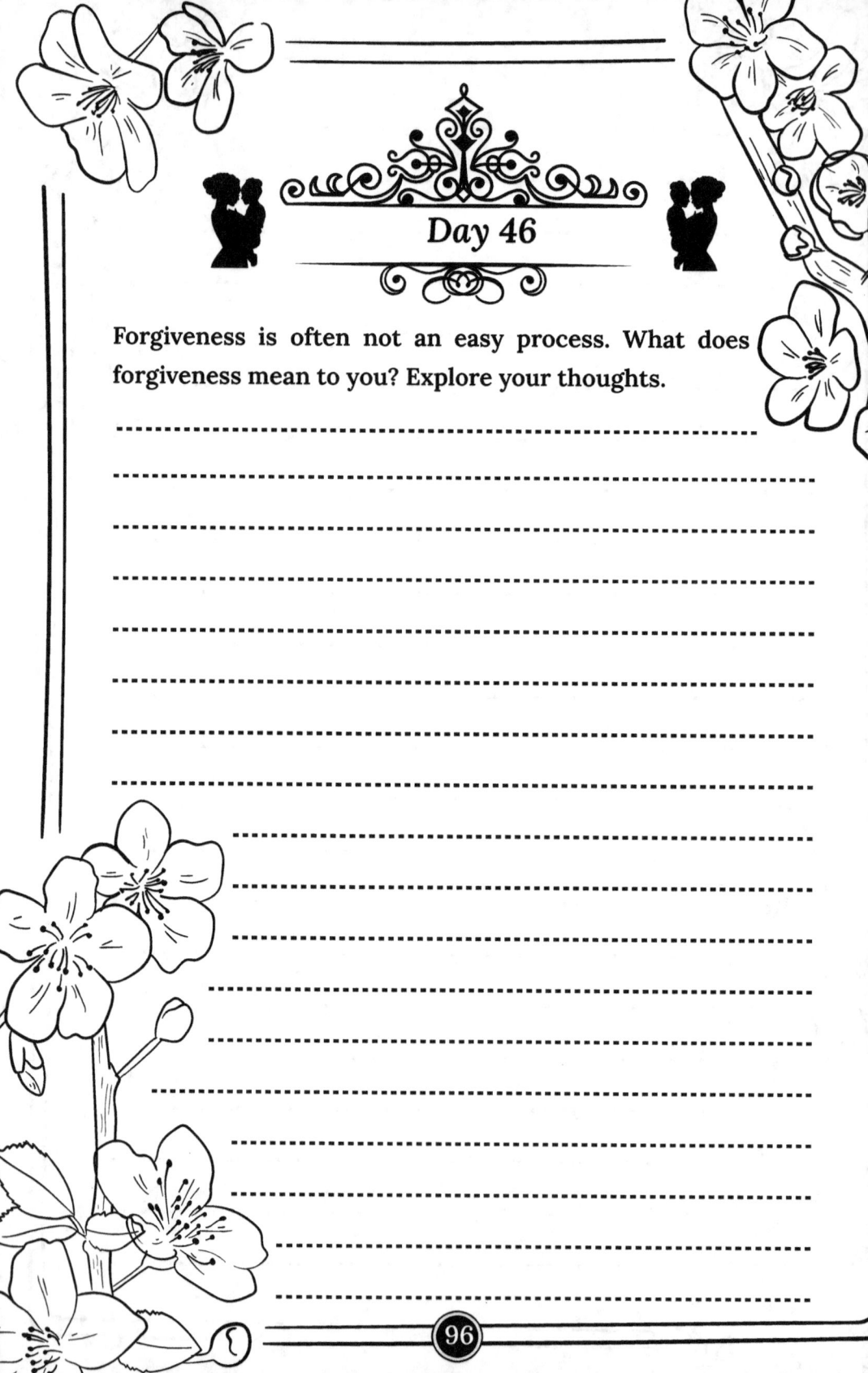

Day 46

Forgiveness is often not an easy process. What does forgiveness mean to you? Explore your thoughts.

Day 47

Are you the generational curse breaker? What do you want to change?

Day 48

Write a letter to your future self about your healing journey. Re-visit it every day for encouragement.

....

....

....

....

....

....

....

....

....

....

....

....

....

....

....

....

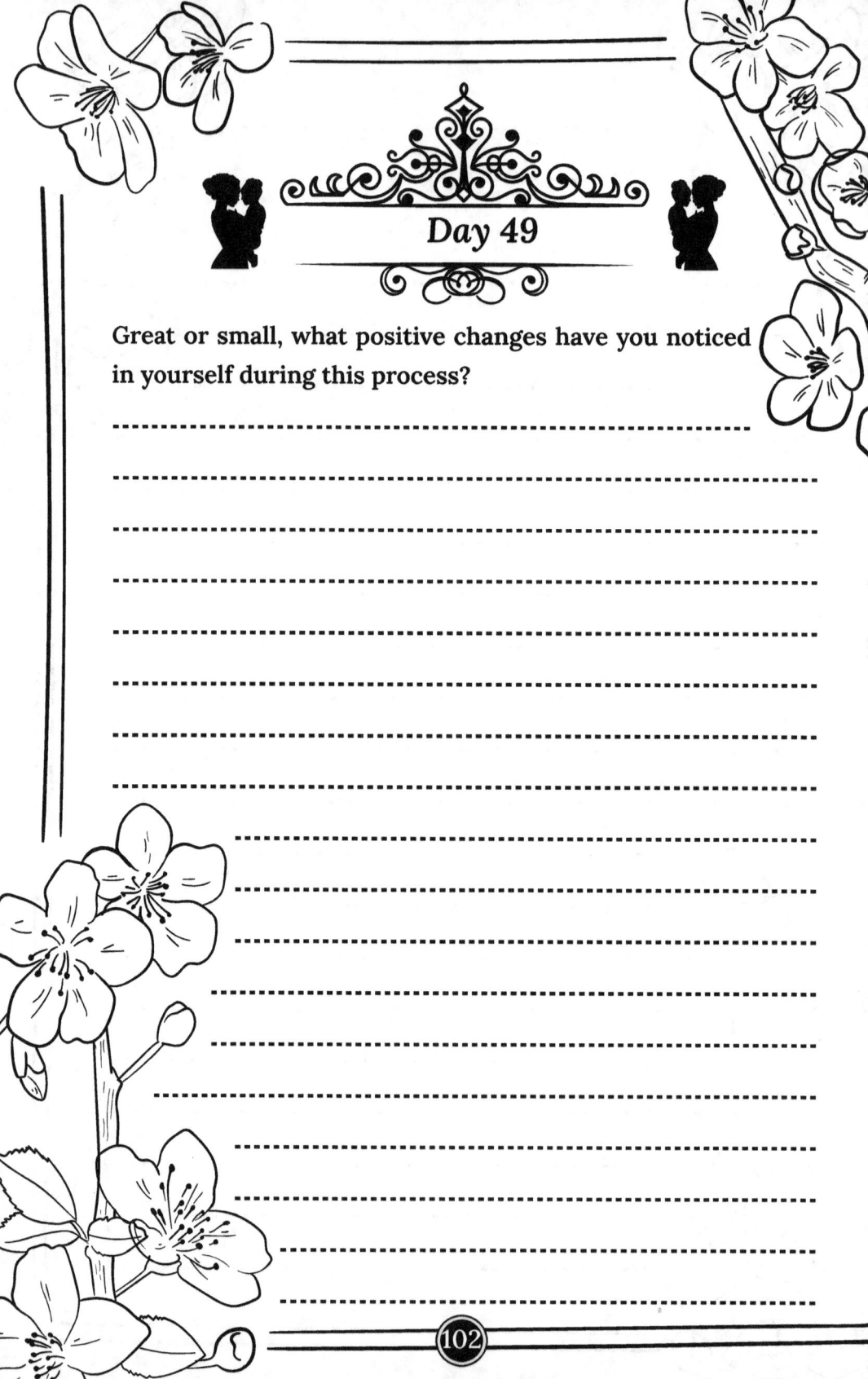

Day 49

Great or small, what positive changes have you noticed in yourself during this process?

Day 50

Create a list of goals for your emotional well-being moving forward.

....

....

....

....

....

....

....

....

....

....

....

....

....

....

....

Reflections of
Gratitude

Day 51

Reflecting on your journey so far. Where do you see the most significant area of improvement?

....
....
....
....
....
....
....
....
....
....
....
....
....
....
....
....

Day 52

Write about the most significant change you've experienced while on this 60-day journal.

....
....
....
....
....
....
....
....
....
....
....
....
....
....
....
....
....

Day 53

List three things you are grateful for in your relationship with your mother.

....

....

....

....

....

....

....

....

....

....

....

....

....

....

....

....

....

Day 54

Describe a recent moment of connection with your mother. Has it improved since your journey began?

Day 55

How have your perceptions of your mother changed since the day of journaling?

....
....
....
....
....
....
....
....
....
....
....
....
....
....
....
....

Day 56

Are you the generational curse breaker? What do you want to change?

Day 57

Have you identified what support you need moving forward? What does that look like to you?

....

....

....

....

....

....

....

....

....

....

....

....

....

....

....

....

Day 58

Reflect on how this journey has impacted your self-identity.

Day 59

Write your mother a letter of love and appreciation.

....
....
....
....
....
....
....
....
....
....
....
....
....
....
....
....
....

Day 60

Celebrate your journey! What are your takeaways, and how will you continue to grow?

Congratulations on Your Journey!

Congratulations on completing this healing journal. Reflecting on your relationship with your mother and any resulting wounds is a significant accomplishment.

Over 60 days, you've courageously faced your emotions, recognized your experiences, and embraced the healing journey. Every prompt, reflection, and exercise has contributed to your self-discovery and growth.

As you finish this chapter, remember that healing is a continuous journey. The knowledge and lessons you have gained will continue to influence your path ahead. Embrace the strength you have developed and carry it with you as you transition into your next phase of life.

Celebrate your resilience, honor your progress, and recognize the bravery it takes to confront your wounds. You are worthy of love, healing, and a future filled with possibilities.

Thank you for allowing this journal to be a part of your journey. May you nurture your spirit and cultivate healing in all areas of your life.

With heartfelt congratulations,

Dr. Kellie Diane

www.ingramcontent.com/pod-product-compliance
Lightning Source LLC
Chambersburg PA
CBHW071009120626
46546CB00003B/1010